LEICESTER LEICESTERSHIRE RUTLAND

PAINTINGS AND SKETCHES BY DOUGLAS SMITH

LEICESTER LEICESTERSHIRE RUTLAND

PAINTINGS AND SKETCHES BY DOUGLAS SMITH

Other books by the same author

TUSCANY Paintings and sketches	ISBN 0-9538124-3-X
FRANCE Paintings and sketches	ISBN 0-9538124-1-3
LEICESTER Paintings and sketches	ISBN 0-9538124-2-1
ARCHITECTURE INTERIOR LANDSCAPE	ISBN 0-9538124-0-5
HOTEL RESTAURANT DESIGN	ISBN 0-435-86501-3

Acknowledgements

This book is dedicated to a unique area of England
Leicester
Leicestershire
Rutland

I would like to thank all those who have suggested and encouraged me to publish this book. To Her Grace the Duchess of Rutland for writing the Foreword. To Lord Attenborough who wrote the Foreword to the Leicester book that forms part of this book. To Edward Moody for the graphic design. To Traphouse Design & Reproduction Limited and to the Leicester Mercury for scanning the paintings and drawings with great skill.

I am indebted to Richard Float for advice on the text. To Hilary Smith, Janey Hawkins, Shirley Smith and Veronica Rawson for their editing and typing skills, who have put me right when I have got it wrong.

I am pleased to acknowledge the following sources for the quotations.

Attenborough, Lord Richard; Browne, Kenneth; Eliot, T S; Environ; Gandhi, Mahotma; Goethe; Helman, Louis; Hockney, David; Hoskins, W G; Pevsner, Nicholas; Schumacher, E F; Report under W K Smigielski; Stewart, Mandy; Taylor, Michael; and 'The Quality of Leicester'; Trueman, A E.

Leicester Leicestershire Rutland
Paintings and Sketches by Douglas Smith

Published in the United Kingdom 2005
Douglas Smith Stimson Partnership Limited
53 Spencefield Lane,
Leicester. LE5 6HH

Graphic Design
Edward Moody Design
169 Knighton Road,
Leicester LE2 3TS

Printed and bound in the United Kingdom by Polar Print Group Limited

ISBN 0-9538124-4-8

Contents

Preface

Leicester market that has been thriving since the late 13th century and is one of the focal points of the city

'We shall not cease from exploration
And the end of all our exploring
Will be to arrive where we started
And know the place for the first time.'

T S Eliot

The title reflects my aim to review, update and condense the contents of the original publication 'Leicester, Paintings and sketches' (now out of print) as part one of this book. Part two sets the city in its context and extends the area to cover Leicestershire and Rutland.

I find the challenge irresistible to record by brushstroke, capturing a sense of place, the buildings and landscape of this area. The intension has been to search for the quality of the subject and at times overlooking distracting elements and even slightly emphasizing parts to create the lasting memory of a scene. It is the vision that is important; Turner from time to time modified and did not slavishly copy every detail to create his wonderful views. For me it is to capture the beautiful buildings, in the evocative mood when the light is right. The book concentrates on the visual qualities and is not a history or a guide.

It is a poignant time at the beginning of the new millennium, to look back as well as forward without preconceived ideas, to cherish the good old and search out the new in the extended area of study.

However familiar you are with Leicester, Leicestershire and Rutland, nothing fascinates more than by looking at the area through other eyes. My purpose is therefore to stimulate a re examination of our rich heritage, old and new, at a pivotal time in history.

Foreword
by the Duchess of Rutland

The Duchess' Spring Garden at Belvoir Castle

When I first came to Leicestershire with my husband-to-be, now the Duke of Rutland, I was overwhelmed by the beauty of the landscape and the history contained in its wonderful buildings and city scenes.

In this evocative book Douglas Smith has captured the essence of all this and given us a unique flavour of a very special part of England.

I do hope that you will enjoy it as much as I have; it will live on my bookshelf and be a frequent reminder of the wonderful part of the country we live in.

Emma Rutland

Her Grace the Duchess of Rutland

The foreword by Lord Attenborough CBE to Leicester, Paintings and sketches

I grew up in Leicester from the age of seven. As a result, my formative years were spent amongst the scenes and buildings depicted in this enchantingly informative book. It evokes so many personal memories of places and people I knew well during those early years of my life. It will, I'm sure, offer a fascination for countless others who experience the joy of looking through it.

Douglas Smith has captured a love of Leicester which reflects its historic past, rejoices in the diversity of its present and heralds its optimism for the future.

I am immensely grateful to Douglas for presenting the images and the 'spirit' of Leicester within these pages for us all to enjoy.

Richard Attenborough

The Cathedral Church of St. Martin is substantially a Victorian Church of the 1860s

Introduction

London Road entering the city with the long distant view to Charnwood Forest

This is the fourth book in the series of Paintings and Sketches, the first one being 'France' followed by 'Leicester' and then 'Tuscany'. The new book covers Leicester, Leicestershire and Rutland, and hence retains Leicester as part one forming a second edition to the original publication. Part two covers the two counties and sets the city in its surroundings.

The underlying geology moulds the scenery of the two counties and could be said to mirror the primary geology of England. One of the prominent geological facts is the diagonal line from south west to north east known as the great 'Stone Belt' from Portland Bill to the Wash and Yorkshire coast. A clay strip follows the same line and there is a dramatic change of rock in the North West where we find the granite and slate of the 'Lake District'. Here we find the same pattern occurs. The oolitic limestone in East Leicestershire and Rutland provides the stone and is the predominant building material for walls and roofs. The clays of the Soar Valley were in plentiful supply for the brick industry that sprang up and became the principal building material. Again a dramatic change takes place in West Leicestershire, where the granite rock and slate of the Charnwood Forest are used for buildings, influencing the design of building in this area. The landscape changes and is in marked contrast to other parts of the counties as the rugged outcrop surfaces in a dramatic way to expose some of the oldest rock to be seen in the world.

Following the 'Industrial Revolution', the plentiful supply of bricks at low prices has blurred the relationship between the natural material of the scenery and in many ways the quality of the ordinary building in the towns and villages. However, Rutland to a greater extent has resisted the use of non-indigenous material.

St. Margaret's Church seen from the inner ring road

The icons of Jewry Wall Museum and St. Nicholas' Church seen from the road of St. Nicholas Circle. The foundation of the nave of the church is Saxon

Leicester is my adopted city, where I arrived in the middle of the twentieth century to study for my second degree at the School of Architecture. I was an undergraduate at Cheltenham School of Art for my first degree after spending a year studying painting, sculpture and pottery. Leicester is a tantalisingly large city, which is visually small in scale for its size and with a fascinating history extending back further than most industrial towns. Its steady growth has left no grand plan or dominant architectural style. Yet, there are pockets of exceptional visual quality, with the significant ones being the Roman remains and a fine adjacent museum. The Guildhall and churches of St. Nicholas and

The Magazine Gateway on the central carriageway
of the inner ring road

Leicester Prison from the inner ring road

St. Mary de Castro, the Castle and the Newarke are landmarks of Roman and Medieval Leicester. Other nationally significant sites are the Georgian New Walk, the twentieth century Department of Engineering for the University of Leicester and the National Space Centre.

My working life was centred on the city with an architectural and landscape practice spanning the last four decades of the twentieth century. Our office was near to Holy Trinity Church, centrally located close to New Walk and the Museum that includes some fine art and natural history collections. The Victorian Gallery in the Museum is a beautiful venue for various meetings including the Literary & Philosophical Society founded in 1835 and the Leicester Decorative Fine Arts Society-a branch of NADFAS. In addition, it provides a good setting for Chamber Music, lunchtime concerts and more recently the Leicester International Music Festival.

The start of the new millennium stimulated thoughts of the future and the need for bench marks from which to begin. The selection in this book is my personal choice and does not claim to be a history or an inclusive record. It is my vision of Leicester at this time. Others will have a different vision but this book should encourage the reader to explore the city and come to their own conclusion.

For twelve years, we had the privilege of living in the 'White House', designed in 1896 by Ernest Gimson, who was a member of the Arts and Craft Movement; it was an important building heralding the modern movement. On many occasions, I have been asked by visitors from far and near to see the house and other Leicester landmark buildings. Hence, this book at the beginning of the third millennium, is my choice of buildings and places, some obvious, some less obvious.

Leicester Cathedral

Leicester

Leicester is a vibrant city that has adapted to the considerable population changes of the second half of the 20th century. Proactive initatives, not only by the City Council, but by all the major institutions have made it a truly multi cultural city.

The strategy statement of the City Council at the start of the 21st century has two fine quotations both to consolidate the initiatives to date and the challenges for the future by including the great wisdom of Mahatma Gandhi

No culture can live, if it attempts to be exclusive.'

It also includes the words of Goethe

'…are so inclined to content themselves with what is commonest; the spirit and the senses so easily grow dead to the impressions of the beautiful and perfect, that every one should study, by all methods, to nourish in his (or her) mind the facility of feeling these things…For this reason, one ought every day at least, to hear a little song, read a good poem, see a fine picture, and, if possible, to speak a few reasonable words'.

There are several techniques available to look at the material fabric of a city. In my experience computers with virtual reality have limitations. I like the results of David Hockney experimenting with the 'joiner' photographs. Firstly, it made artists think again about alternatives to the one point perspective and secondly, and perhaps more significantly, it adds time into the sense of place. The 'joiner' photograph taken of the Museum, the movement along New Walk and the Regency Cottages

Sketch of Museum, Regency Houses and New Walk

succeeds for me, whereas the 'fish eye' lens would distort the scene. However, Hockney found the camera had limitations and stated, 'Painting can give you far, far more and I am concerned most about painting as a depiction of the visible world.' It is difficult to visualise the relationship between New Walk, the Museum and the Regency Houses without this technique.

We must welcome and be excited by the shock of the new. In the past, society not only accepted dramatic changes of style but also actively demanded new fashions. At any given time, the number of new buildings in relation to the existing stock is quite small. Leicester has a long and fascinating history

King Street vista to Holy Trinity Church
flanked by the Crescent and Crescent
Cottages in the 'joiner' photograph

Sketch of King Street vista

Jaguar Showroom for W E Sturgess 2001
designed by Douglas Smith Stimson Pts. Ltd,
Executive architects Pick Everard

Braunstone Leisure Centre 2004
designed by S and P Architects

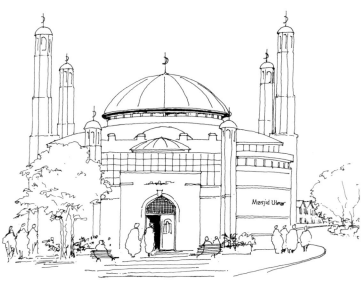

Masjia Ulmar Mosque 2000
designed by Kent Porter Warren Architects

seen through the buildings, townscape and developments that have taken place. The needs of people change and buildings must be adapted for new uses. Permanently redundant buildings deteriorate quickly and are targets for vandals and therefore should be avoided. Inevitably, some fine buildings have been lost. This has happened throughout history, perhaps no more so than in Victorian times. In my opinion, conservation is not just preservation. The Conservation Area Policy must conserve the best, where possible maintaining the character that made it so, but encouraging the new to enrich our heritage for future generations and not being afraid to demolish where necessary.   ·

Road layouts have changed the face of Leicester and from the car, fleeting glimpses are seen: for example the Roman Museum, Jewry Wall, St. Nicholas Church, the Magazine Gateway, the Prison and St. Margarets Church.

On the approaches to the city there are three recent buildings that are landmarks, one from the M1/M69, Centre 21 Fosse Park on the A5460 is the Jaguar Showrooms of W E Sturgess & Sons, designed by Douglas Smith Stimson Partnership with executive architects Pick Everard. Another on the B667 Evington Lane is the imposing silhouette and interesting building of the Masjid Ulmar Mosque designed by Kent Porter Warren Architects. Finally on the A47 and completed in 2004, is the flagship Braunstone Leisure Centre by S and P Architects for the major regeneration programme for Braunstone.

Towards the end of the twentieth century, the scale of buildings has had the biggest impact on our cities and towns. No longer is the tower or steeple of the church the dominant feature. A challenge came from high rise blocks of offices and flats. Le Corbusier, the Swiss/French architect actively promoted the idea of large buildings in parkland as the solution to the needs of population growth. The large complex building like his L'Unité d'Habitation in Marseilles was constructed with the shopping street on one floor. It was not enthusiastically accepted and when applied on a smaller scale it was a disaster. People needed to get out of the building and to have the opportunity to meet, exchange ideas or chat as they moved in the town. Leicester had only a few tower blocks but in many cases they have proved difficult for the City Council tenants, resulting in the demolition of some of them and replacement by more popular and user friendly low rise housing.

Time scale has progressively influenced construction: before the first millennium, it was not a significant factor. In the middle of the second millennium, things started to change and its effect accelerated. Then it became interrelated with cost, and in the last century ever more so, due to the significant and sometimes catastrophic impact on cash flow when a building is completed late. Faster,

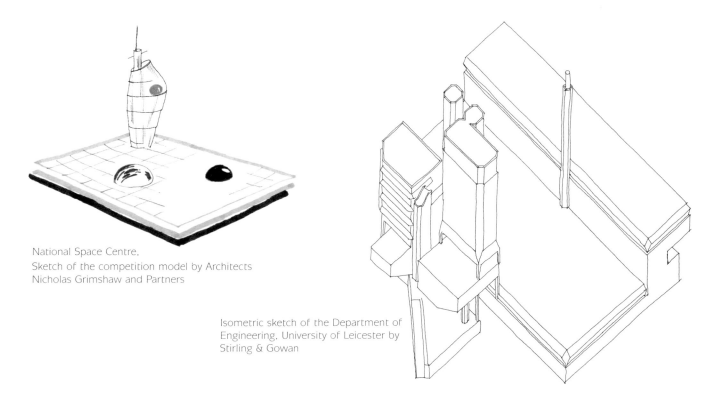

National Space Centre,
Sketch of the competition model by Architects
Nicholas Grimshaw and Partners

Isometric sketch of the Department of
Engineering, University of Leicester by
Stirling & Gowan

cheaper building is a temptation for the unscrupulous developer to exploit. In real estate land values become increasingly significant and represent a high percentage of development costs. The now familiar saying 'location, location, location' is the essential factor for success.

A large scheme can destroy the character and scale of many historic towns. The friendly familiar size of the building frontage of about fifteen strides gives a comfortable rhythm to the eye. If large groups of such properties are purchased and redeveloped as one building, the impact is likely to be disastrous. 'Small is Beautiful' in the words of Schumacher but this sadly is unlikely to satisfy modern criteria.

Leicester suffered in the second half of the twentieth century when the underpass with St. Nicholas' Circle was constructed. It shattered the oldest part of the town, destroying its scale and integrity. However, bold planning decisions were made to save parts of the city for future generations. The character of the Market was preserved by the retention of the facades to Market Place when Marshall and Snelgrove Store on Gallowtree Gate was redeveloped. In Town Hall Square the Sun Alliance Building, now a bank, was saved from demolition. The inner ring road was originally designed to cut through the Crescent and New Walk, but, with further discussion leading to greater sensitivity, it was eventually re-routed as Waterloo Way passing under New Walk.

Cressida Place, Braunstone by Architect William Butterfield

St Peter's Braunstone

The University of Leicester in the 60's and 70's led the way with some landmark modern buildings, with the Department of Engineering being the outstanding example. The City Council, in conjunction with the charity Environ, worked hard to make Leicester the first Environment City. They spearheaded the world sustainability programme in the city and started to encourage other towns and cities. The Queens Building of De Montfort University is a pioneer in energy saving, encapsulating the best features of environmental design.

Leicester has always had an ethnic community which increased considerably when in the early 1970s a high percentage of displaced Asian people came to the city from Uganda. The city became multicultural, Belgrave Road being the 'Bond Street' for silk and gold in the country. Mosques and temples are now part of the cityscape.

At the beginning of the third millennium, Leicester has a significant new complex, the National Space Centre. An educational, science-based initiative by Leicester University and the City Council where undergraduates, school children and the public can experience the many aspects of space exploration. The good news for the future is the approval and start of the exciting new theatre designed by the award winning architects Rafael Vinoly of New York.

The Roman Jewry Wall and St. Nicholas Church seen
from Vaughan College

The heart of the Roman and Medieval Town

The structures which interest me date from when the Romans founded the town and named it "Ratae Coritanorum" soon after the invasion by Claudius in A.D. 43. Substantial buildings were constructed and new discoveries occur when excavations take place in the old town area and along or adjacent to the Roman roads. The surviving Jewry Wall and its foundations have been successfully exploited and incorporated into the Jewry Wall Museum. It forms part of the Vaughan College development of the University of Leicester designed in 1962 by the architect Trevor Dannatt. For me, the museum building captures the sense of place with the Forum. The Jewry Wall for a time formed the foundation of the end of St. Nicholas Church, which may well have preserved it, preventing others from using the materials for their buildings. An interesting spatial relationship between the college, the wall and the church has been created. The church of St. Nicholas has a nave that dates from Anglo-Saxon times and is the oldest city church. In the central Norman tower, there are re-used Roman tiles.

The medieval town was built over the Roman settlement, but in those days the ground level of towns often rose in the region of a foot each century due to the consolidation of rubbish. However, this helped to preserve the earlier remains. The buildings and network of roads that developed had some fine buildings, many of which remain. Unfortunately, the cohesive pattern of this part of the city was shattered in the 1960's by the construction of St. Nicholas Circle and the underpass. Mr Konrad Smigielski, the first planner to be appointed, saved many parts of the city. Examples of these are the retention of the rear facade of the Market Place buildings, which is a visually important part of the enclosing space of the Market; the Crescent, which was saved from demolition for the ring road; and finally, the preservation of the integrity of Town Hall Square by obtaining 'listing' of the Sun Alliance

St. Mary de Castro with Turret Gateway
in the foreground

St Mary de Castro, Norman porch, late 12th century

St Mary de Castro Church
with the Norman doorway
visible from the pedestrian
bridge of St Nicholas Circle

Building thus preventing demolition. However, he failed to see the impact of the scale of some of the new buildings and the feeling of isolation and separation, which the underpass created in the City.

Leicester was late in becoming a City (1919) and for much of its history was ecclesiastically in the See of Peterborough. It is therefore not surprising that it was a relatively small town until the industrial revolution, with no great Medieval Church or Cathedral to dominate the town. The Cathedral Church of St. Martin is a Victorian building and was given Cathedral status in 1927.

Guildhall 1343 a fine medieval
building of national significance.
It also has an interesting courtyard.

The main hall of the Guildhall, a beautiful example of timber engineering of the period

Wyggeston's House. A fine example of a sixteenth century medieval timbered hall behind a later Georgian frontage

The boundaries of the old town are clearly defined. In the West by the river; in the North by the Roman Centre; in the South the castle and St. Mary de Castro; in the North East corner is St. Margarets Church and to the South East the market place. Leicester can be proud of its Guildhall (1343) which is intact and of national importance, a fine building surviving from the medieval period. Constructed of timber with an impressive hall it exploits timber technology of the time. Close by is a little gem – Wyggeston's House, another fine medieval timber building behind a Georgian façade. Sadly at this time it is not in use, but until recently it housed Leicester Museums Costume Collection.

The great hall of the Castle survives from 1168 and it became the assize court in 1273. It continued as a court until the early 1980s. The mound is the most dominant feature seen from the river and canal.

It is interesting to find that the High Cross placed at the centre of an important market town survives from the Middle Ages. It has been repositioned from High Cross Street to the corner of the market place at the head of Cheapside close to the Clock Tower.

The shop in the Market Place, formerly Pearce and Sons, has seventeenth century gables and a fine Edwardian shopfront. An original timber-frame, beams and roof trusses dating from the fifteenth century were exposed by a fire and now form part of the sales area.

The Town Hall 1876 designed by
F J Hames, is in scale with the
relatively small square that is
dominated by the bronze fountain

Leicester has a long history of markets and one has flourished in Market Place for seven hundred years. The Corn Exchange 1850 by William Flint is in the background. Later additions, tower and Venetian style double flight staircase 1855 by F W Ordish

The City

There are two large spaces in the centre. One is the market with a history reaching back 700 years and the other is Town Hall Square.

First, the Market Place as seen today is the result of an intensive study and controversy in the 1960's under W K Smigielski. The resulting report states:

'The main idea of this scheme is the modernisation of an open market in the heart of a prosperous industrial city. The open market, although the oldest form of shopping and considered by many as a medieval anachronism, can play a vital role in the life of a modern city along with the retail shop, department store and supermarket. The open market has remained in its present position with new roofs over the stalls and there is a small paved forecourt in front of the Corn Exchange formed.'

The Corn Exchange by William Flint in 1850 was once the Market Hall. The imposing double flight staircase in Venetian style and the clock tower were added later by F W Ordish in 1855.

Second, the Town Hall and the Square with its bronze fountain in the centre, flanked by paving and grass, creates a gathering place in the city. Both were designed by a local architect F J Hames and built between 1873-76. Pevsner states: *'Fortunately the Council were lucky in their choice and ended up with a design remarkably free and comfortable for its date and official purpose – in fact with the first Queen-Anne-style municipal buildings.'*

The City Rooms 1790's, a fine Georgian building
by John Johnson

The first floor of the City Rooms has a
beautiful Georgian interior. Unfortunately,
a more recent treatment of the ceiling
detracts a little

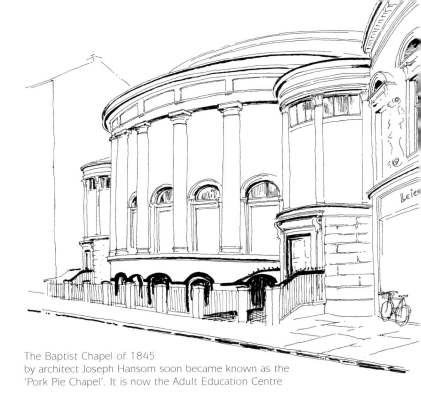

The Baptist Chapel of 1845
by architect Joseph Hansom soon became known as the
'Pork Pie Chapel'. It is now the Adult Education Centre

The Turkey Café on Granby Street designed by
Arthur Wakerley in 1910. A fascinating use of
faience tiles exploiting the theme of the turkey

Leicester fortuitously has the City Rooms, which form the finest Georgian building in Leicester designed by John Johnson in 1792. Built originally as a hotel and county ballroom for those attending Leicester Races, it was never used as a hotel.

An interesting building is to be found on Belvoir Street. Designed in 1845 by architect Joseph Hansom of the London Hansom cab fame, it was originally a Baptist Chapel but later became the Adult Education Centre. Its shape resulted in the building being referred to as the 'Pork Pie Chapel'.

A landmark because of its unusual design is the Turkey Café on Granby Street, by local architect Arthur Wakerley in 1910. It has a tile and stone facade with turkey cock features at parapet and ground floor levels.

Silver Arcade 1899 designed by Amos Hall

St Martin's Square

Alexandra House has fine terracotta detailing

An interesting Victorian shopping arcade is to be found in Silver Street, designed by Amos Hall. A large lantern light is the culmination of the three storey cast iron galleries.

When constructing the large shopping complex of the Shires the High Street frontage was retained, maintaining the original scale of the street. An interesting high level view is seen from the pedestrian bridge of St. Nicholas Circle.

A start has been made on the ambitious plans to transform the St George's area into a major arts venue including the new theatre. There are two existing buildings of significance. The striking corner site of the Odeon designed by Robert Bullivant of Architects Harry Weedon in 1939 is a thirties celebration of cinemas in pre-war Britain, now reopened as 'The Athena' entertainment venue. Adjacent is Alexandra House, designed as a bootlace warehouse by Edward Burgess in 1897. The detail of the terracotta façade is a remarkable example of financial investment in an early industrial building.

The Newarke is on the fringe of the medieval town. There are significant buildings dating back to that period, Turret Gateway, built about 1423, together with St. Mary de Castro form a familiar icon of Leicester. Prince Rupert entered the City after the Siege in 1645 and it is frequently referred to as Rupert's Gate. Chantry House and some later cottages flank the walk through to the church. Charities

Exchange Building Rutland Street, Grade II listed. Original Architect Stockdale Harrison, enlightened roof extension by Allison Pike Architects.

House built by William Wyggeston in 1513 and Skeffington House built in 1600 are now part of the Newarke Houses Museum.

The Magazine Gateway is early fifteenth century and originally the entrance to this 'new work'; hence the name 'The Newarke'. The gate itself acquired its name much later because of being used as a magazine during the Civil War. The inner ring road has isolated it on the central reservation with access from the pedestrian underpass.

Bede Island area was a successful Leicester City Challenge development breathing life into a depressed part of the city. West Bridge Place, situated on the Canal facing Castle Gardens, is a landmark complex centred on the original Pex Factory designed by William Flint in 1850 and incorporated into the new offices for the Land Registry.

New Walk was created in 1785 in the Georgian period to provide Leicester with a route to perambulate from the heart of the city. It terminated at the Racecourse, which is now Victoria Park. The walk attracted residences along its frontage and it soon became a desirable area, but went into decline post Second World War. Fortunately it survived and when it was made a conservation area, a programme of restoration commenced. For me, it is a unique example of 'creative townscape'

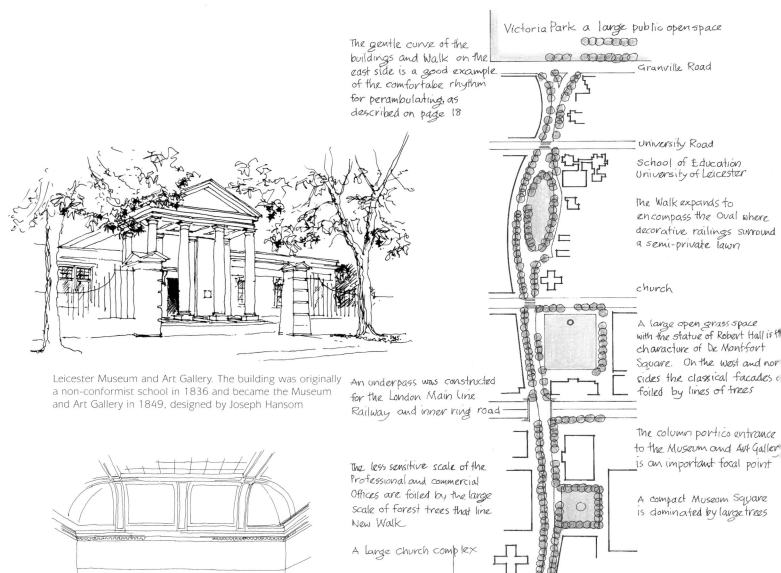

Leicester Museum and Art Gallery. The building was originally a non-conformist school in 1836 and became the Museum and Art Gallery in 1849, designed by Joseph Hansom

The Victorian Gallery at the New Walk Museum and Art Gallery

The gentle curve of the buildings and Walk on the east side is a good example of the comfortable rhythm for perambulating, as described on page 18

An underpass was constructed for the London Main Line Railway and inner ring road

The less sensitive scale of the Professional and commercial offices are foiled by the large scale of forest trees that line New Walk

A large church complex

North

Victoria Park a large public open space

Granville Road

University Road

School of Education University of Leicester

The Walk expands to encompass the Oval where decorative railings surround a semi-private lawn

church

A large open grass space with the statue of Robert Hall is the character of De Montfort Square. On the west and north sides the classical facades are foiled by lines of trees

The column portico entrance to the Museum and Art Gallery is an important focal point

A compact Museum Square is dominated by large trees

King Street

Leicester City Council Offices New Walk Centre

New Walk.
A landscape study based on a diagrammatic plan

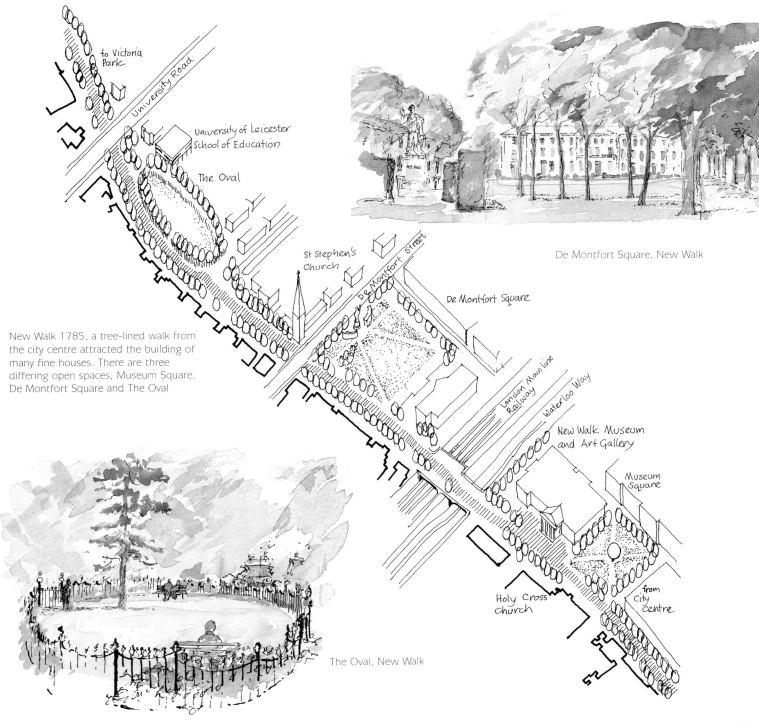

to Victoria Park

University Road

University of Leicester
School of Education

The Oval

St Stephen's
Church

De Montfort Street

De Montfort Square

De Montfort Square, New Walk

New Walk 1785, a tree-lined walk from
the city centre attracted the building of
many fine houses. There are three
differing open spaces, Museum Square,
De Montfort Square and The Oval

London Main line
Railway

Waterloo Way

New Walk Museum
and Art Gallery

Museum
Square

Holy Cross
Church

from
city
centre

The Oval, New Walk

33

The Georgian Crescent and Crescent Cottages at the south end of King Street, near to Holy Trinity Church

consisting of a linear walk with three contrasting spaces linked by an avenue of fine mature trees.

First, there is the compact Museum Square, enclosed by Georgian and Regency buildings on two sides with the Museum and New Walk completing the enclosure.

De Montfort Square is the largest of the three spaces, where in living memory sheep grazed. It is now a large green space dominated by a statue of Robert Hall. The Church of St. Stephen acts as punctuation to the otherwise domestic scale of the buildings forming the square. The Oval is the third of the open spaces where decorative railings surround a semi-private lawn.

It is a beautiful walk and there are glimpses of modern buildings behind the trees including the School of Education of the University of Leicester which integrates more successfully than some new buildings of earlier developments.

For me, the most significant building in this area is the Leicester Museum and Art Gallery for which the Walk makes a fine setting. The building was first used as a non-conformist school built in 1839. It was adapted to the design of Joseph Hansom for its present use in 1849. The imposing column portico is in scale with the walk. There is a fine collection of paintings and a major ceramics exhibition 'Picasso- The Attenborough Collection'. The Literary & Philosophical Society was instrumental in the formation of the Museum and Art Gallery.

Shop in the Market Place late 19th century
shop front in 17th century gables

The Newarke Houses now Leicester
Museum was originally Chantry House
by William Wyggeston 1513 and then
Skeffington House 1600

The Shires was opened in 1991.
Architects Chapman Taylor and Partners

London Road Station by C. Trubshaw 1892.
A fine example of Victorian architecture in
red brick and sandstone

An interesting vista is to be found at the end of King Street, focused on the spire of Holy Trinity Church and flanked by the Crescent and the Crescent Cottages. Smigielski, who re-routed the inner ring road and conceived the idea of the underpass to preserve the integrity of the New Walk, saved the Georgian terraced houses from demolition. The Crescent and the Cottages that extended into Upper King Street were renovated in the 1970's and now contain business and professional offices. It is a small and beautiful enclave of Georgian and Regency buildings.

An impression of grandeur is experienced when entering the city from the south after passing the racecourse and the Botanic Gardens of the University of Leicester. London Road (A6) runs between fine forest trees and is studded by large houses that are set in big gardens. Many of the houses have been developed by Housing Associations; but some are now used for professional and semi-professional use. The scale and modelling of the original dwellings have been retained.

The leafy suburb extends to Victoria Park. The words in 'The Quality of Leicester' describe the park perfectly for me. 'Victoria Park is very different from the other late nineteenth century parks in the city. There was little attempt to create a picturesque landscape with ornamental trees, rockeries or formal flower beds as there was at Abbey Park. The quality of Victoria Park lies in its size and openness, broken only by avenues of trees. It feels expansive and refreshing. On Sunday mornings the Park is colourful and active with football matches. A summer's evening sees Victoria Park alive with games of cricket. As dusk falls on a winter's afternoon the Park is at its most impressive, the buildings around the edge lit up and traffic, for once an asset, giving a sense of buzzing activity beyond the open space.'

The eye is attracted to the sensitively designed Park gates and the adjacent Lodges, the work of Sir Edwin Lutyens in 1926, in combination with the formal approach to the War Memorial also designed by Lutyens.

At this point, the London Road changes to an urban road but with long distance views over the city that is very conspicuous when the sun highlights the mauve tinged rock and bracken of the Charnwood Forest beyond.

Joseph Goddard designed the Clock Tower in 1868.
Samuel Barfield created the statues of city figures –
Simon de Montfort, William of Wigston (Wyggeston),
Sir Thomas White and Gabriel Newton

White House by Ernest Gimson in 1897 was in my opinion a timeless design

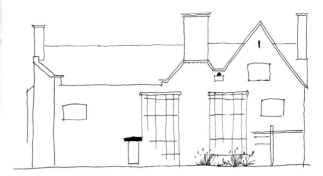

Great Meeting Unitarian Church complex

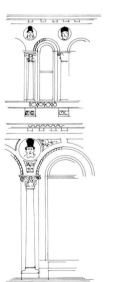

Top Hat Terrace, London Road. 1864

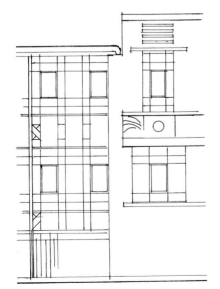

Originally the Goddards factory, Nelson Street, by Bedingfield & Grundy 1932, now a solicitors office

A fine timber framed and clad Industrial warehouse in Butt Close Lane

West Bridge Place, one of the Gateways to Bede Island, the successful City
Challenge Development. The original Pex building 1850, is by William Flint

De Montfort Hall 1913 by Shirley Harrison

A solicitor's office occupies Top Hat Terrace of 1864 where the sculptural heads of the top hatted gentlemen add to the charm of numbers 119 and 117A London Road.

London Road Station, built by the Victorians for the old Midland Railway, is reminiscent in colour and material of the grand St. Pancras Chambers in London where this line terminates. Two cast iron telephone boxes outside the station have been listed; these were designed by Giles Gilbert Scott in 1935.

Tower blocks have been built around this space but it is the rich modelling and interesting corner design of the YMCA building that attracts the eye of the artist architect.

In the leafy suburbs of Knighton and Stoneygate, there are glimpses of the work of architects Barradale and Goddard but I will focus on the work of Ernest Gimson. The 'White House' built in 1897 for his brother Arthur is an ageless, honest building of beautiful proportion and simplicity. The windowless gable is like the bow of a ship gliding out to the Avenue. Superb detailing reflects the influence of the Arts and Craft movement to which Gimson contributed significantly. In the Charnwood Forest there are four cottages designed by Gimson for the family.

Panoramic view from Victoria Park

Left to right: Department of Engineering by Stirling and Gowan, Attenborough Tower by Sir Philip Dawson
(Arup Associates), Charles Wilson Building Sir Denys Lasdon, low level University buildings by Sir Leslie Martin
and Sir Colin St. John Wilson all part of University of Leicester

The Queen's Building 1993
De Montfort University by
Peake, Short and Ford

Universities

De Montfort University started in 1897 as the first building of further education. The original idea for a College of Art & Technology was debated by the Council in 1895. Two years later the Hawthorn Building, to the design of Perkins Pick, was completed, taking inspiration from the seventeenth century. The old building of the College of Art and Technology was given the status of Polytechnic in 1969. Numerous buildings were added and, in 1992, it became De Montfort University.

The University has grown rapidly. Alan Short and Brian Ford's School of Engineering and Manufacture is a significant new building opened by the Queen and named after her. It explores the Green Agenda and has an integrated design to minimise energy use. In 1993 it was the largest passively ventilated and energy-saving building in Europe. The design challenges modern architectural theory with new ideas.

The Technology, Transfer and Training Centre, designed by Douglas Smith Stimson Partnership Ltd, on the corner of Oxford Street and Bonners Lane is one of the links between commerce, industry and De Montfort University.

The library by Eva Jiricna Architects has a tension fabric structural entrance canopy.

There is an impressive expansion proposal including a Landscape master plan for the campus; for the City it will free the historic Magazine from its isolation by the road pattern and make it part of the new Magazine Square.

Department of Engineering, University of Leicester 1963 by Sir James Stirling and James Gowan.
This building helped to change the face of University buildings from that date

The vision and foresight of some notable Leicester people led to various proposals to establish a University in the City. Eventually, it was the enthusiasm of Dr Astley Clarke, a local physician, with the support of the Literary and Philosophical Society, which led to the founding of the University College in 1921. However, this was only made possible by the generosity of Thomas Fielding Johnson, a local worsted manufacturer, who purchased land on what is now the University Road site, that he gifted for educational purposes.

The new college was established in an existing Georgian building designed by Wallatt and Parsons in 1838 that had served as the Leicester and Rutland Lunatic Asylum until the outbreak of the war in 1914. Following its use as a military hospital, it then lay empty. The first principal was R F Rattray succeeded by F L Attenborough in 1932 and, in turn, by Charles Wilson in 1951. In 1957, the College received full University status by Royal Charter. Today, the original building is the administrative centre of the University. Appropriately, it is named the Fielding Johnson Building.

The rapid expansion of higher education in the 1950s soon made it apparent that there was a need for a master plan to make best use of the undeveloped parts of the site. Professor Sir Leslie Martin was appointed as Consultant and Planning Architect in 1956. Sir Leslie's duties included advising the University on the appointment of architects for the new buildings that were needed to teach and accommodate the much-increased number of students. This resulted in a large number of nationally known architects working on projects at the University, providing Leicester with a 'Tour de Force' of leading edge architecture. Thereby it discarded the noose of the immediate post-war neo classical buildings near to the original buildings and the Georgian style of the original building.

From left to right: Chemistry building 1960 by Architects Co-Partnership
Physics, Bennett Building & Ratray Theatre 1959-65 by Architects Sir Leslie Martin & Sir Colin St John Wilson

In the early 1960s the last remnants of the original interior were converted and modernised when Douglas Smith designed the interior refit and upgrading of the main entrance area. During the work, Sir Fraser Noble, Vice- Chancellor, inquired 'Douglas is everything fine?'

'No' I said, "we need a large picture for the space'.

'The difficulty may be how to find one'.

'Ask your architect to find one', I retorted.

And so the task started to find one within the small budget suggested. It led to the first commission for Bryan Organ, 'The Girl with the Violin', which still dominates the entrance.

For me, the first of the modern buildings is still the outstanding building on the campus. The Department of Engineering 1963 by James Stirling while still in partnership with James Gowan, heralded a transformation of style in University buildings internationally. The functional elements are expressed in a powerful arrangement of volume and the building has attracted the attention of architects from all over the world. Sir Leslie Martin and Sir Colin St John Wilson were responsible for many of the buildings stretching out towards Memorial Walk.

Sir Denys Lasdon designed Charles Wilson Building in 1967. In 1970 Sir Philip Dawson of Arup Associates designed The Attenborough Building named after F L Attenborough, the Principal of the

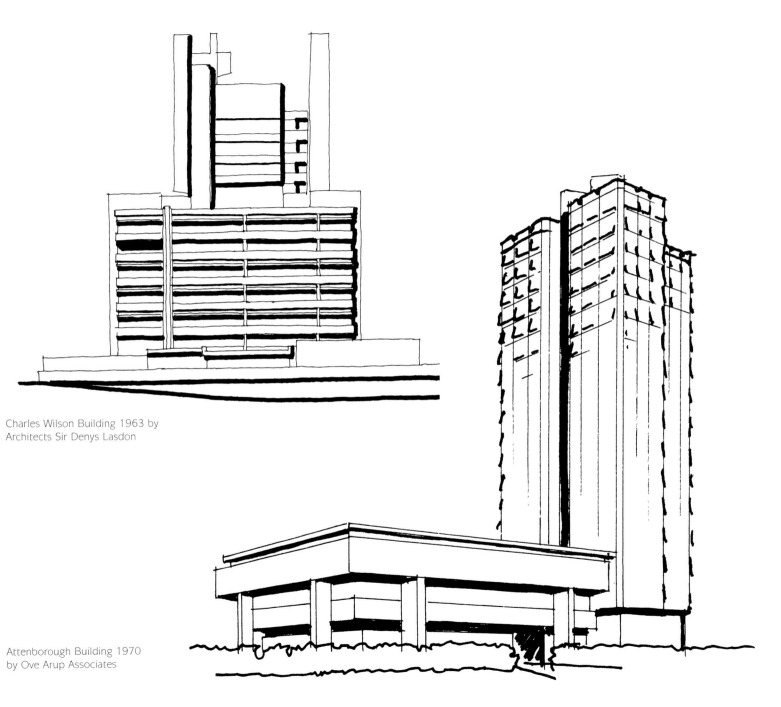

Charles Wilson Building 1963 by
Architects Sir Denys Lasdon

Attenborough Building 1970
by Ove Arup Associates

Vaughan College, University of Leicester 1962
by architect Trevor Dannatt

The Richard Attenborough Centre 1997
by Ian Taylor of Bennett Associates

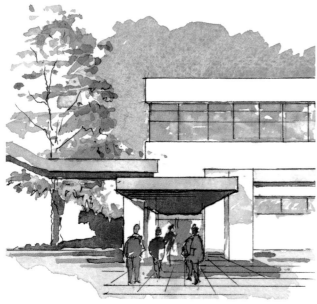

School of Education, University of Leicester 1966
by architect Douglas Smith

Library 1970 by Architects Castle Park Dean Hook

University College 1932 and father of Lord Attenborough and Sir David Attenborough. The University Library by Castle Park Dean Hook is between the Department of Engineering and the Fielding Johnson Building.

There is Café Piazza at the base of the Charles Wilson Building, next to the Bookshop. The café is a small building using the latest structural potential of glass for walls and roof forming a transparent facade facing Victoria Park. Prefabricated timber elements delineate the main space of the café designed by Douglas Smith Stimson Partnership Ltd. 1998.

Towards the end of the twentieth century when Dr. Ken Edwards was Vice-Chancellor, two significant buildings were commenced, one on the edge and the other away from the main campus. Ian Taylor of Bennett Associates won the competition for the Richard Attenborough Centre. This building provides courses in the arts (particularly painting, sculpture, music and dance) which are designed to be suitable for all types of students including and especially those with disabilities. The National Space Centre is also an architectural competition project located at Abbey Meadows. The winning team was Nicholas Grimshaw & Partners and the building was complete in 2001. It facilitates space research, enhances science education in the UK and in addition enables school children and the public to experience the realities of space travel and astronomy by simulation.

The University of Leicester unveiled in 2004 the most ambitious development plan in its history - surpassing the investment that had occurred over the past 40 years.

Ventilating shafts of the Queens Building 1993
by Peake Short & Ford

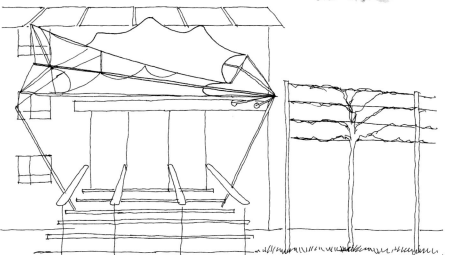

Canopy to Library Entrance
1999 by Eva Jiricna Architects

Technology, Transfer & Training Centre 1995, De Montfort University.
The building is the link with commerce and industry by Douglas
Smith Stimson Partnership Ltd

A short walk in Highfields

Sparkenhoe Community Theatre 2004 by Ash Sakula Architects
St. Peters Church, Highfields
Leicester Synagogue

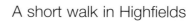

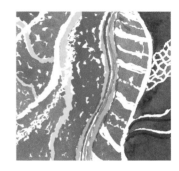

Multi-Cultural City

Leicester has been a multi-cultural city from the establishment of the Roman Settlement. This has enriched the scene starting with the Roman remains, which were described earlier in the book.

The Highfields area has seen many social changes. It consists of large houses built by well to do professionals and industrialists in the nineteenth century. It was to this area that many of the African Caribbean people came but few buildings emerged to change the scene. There is the distinctive dome of the synagogue built in 1898 by Arthur Wakerley. Sadly, the spire of the nearby St. Peters Church of 1878 by architect G E Street has disappeared.

A small project, the Sparkenhoe Community Theatre and Arts Centre, that was conceived by the children at the adjacent school, and designed by Ash Sakula Architects is housed in a transformed 1950's prefab with a large extension. It was the winner of the 2004 East Midlands Architecture Award.

When the Ugandans forced a rapid exit of the Asian Community, many came to Leicester and revitalised sections of declining local industries. There was also at this time an influx of people from the Indian sub-continent.

The Mosque 2000 and St. Philip's Church at
the junction of Evington Lane

Jain Temple, an intricately
sculptured interior

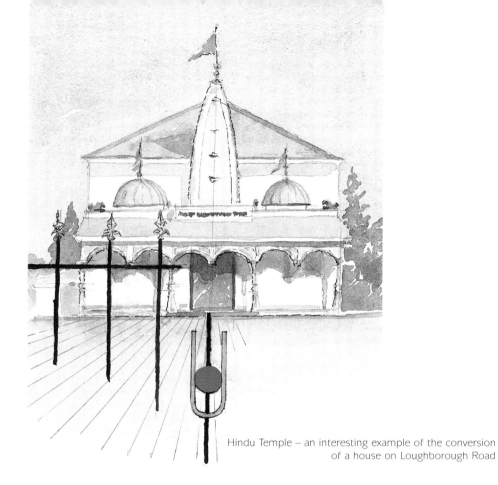

Hindu Temple – an interesting example of the conversion
of a house on Loughborough Road

The numerous religious needs of the newcomers started to impact on the building of Leicester, firstly by modifying the interiors of factories and other buildings to new use but soon more significant changes occurred. There emerged the Jain Centre in 1983 by the conversion of a Congregational Chapel in Oxford Street. The interior became an elaborately carved temple, incorporating marble and stone from India and the exterior was clad in marble. A nineteenth century house on Loughborough Road has been converted to a Hindu Temple.

Across the city new mosques appeared. An interesting juxtaposition occurs in Evington Road, with a new mosque and St. Philips Church.

Belgrave Road has become the 'Bond Street' for silks, gold and silver. There is colour and more colours. The city has spectacular festivals and carnivals where shapes, forms and colour add to the richness of this multi-cultural city.

Evington Church

The striking form of St. Joseph's Church (RC)
1969 at the corner of Goodwood Road &
Uppingham Road. Architect T E Wilson

Outer Leicester

Leicester is in a clay basin of modest size and from time to time, a glimpse of the countryside beyond is seen. Entering the town from the south along London Road at Victoria Park the fine view of the mauve landscape of Charnwood Forest is seen on a clear day. It is an area of ancient rock formations with an interesting history. Again, from the outer ring road near Beaumont Leys, the distinctive landmark of Billesdon Coplow with the lower Fox Covet to the left can be seen. This hill, exposed to the harsh winds from the Russian Urals, has no high landmass to stop their penetrating bite. However, the main reasons to devote a section to outer Leicester are the opportunity it provides to include a number of visually important buildings and to mention the work of Environ. It is a charity with a vision; 'A society where every individual and organisation is contributing to an increasingly sustainable environment.' Its mission is 'To promote locally based change towards sustainable development.' The headquarters is on Western Park; it has had national and international impact. There is much for mankind to consider and then to decide upon taking positive action with the rapidly increasing demand for fresh water, the rise of sea level, population growth world wide and the frightening increase of carbon emissions. The Eco House demonstrates a response to increasing concern about the impact of our life styles on the environment.

Leicester has a green trail along a Riverside Park stretching from Watermead Country Park on the north city boundary over 12 miles to Bluebank Lock in the south, linking the countryside with the heart of Leicester.

There are the old villages of Knighton, Evington, Old Humberstone, Braunstone and Aylestone and in each case the church is an important building. I have restricted my choice to a few examples to give an impression of their diversity.

Water garden with the sunken garden
in the background, Botanic Gardens,
University of Leicester

Sculpture in the garden 2004.
'Regatta' by Sydney Carter with
Beaumont Hall in the distance

Small pavilion in the garden

The Harold Martin Botanic Garden of University of Leicester originated in 1920 when the Botanical Section of the Leicester Literary and Philosophical Society was invited to establish a garden for the College, later to become the University. It moved in 1947 to the present site to vacate land for expansion of the campus. The Oadby site, comprising four houses and gardens, Beaumont, Southmeade, The Knoll and Hastings, were designed by the architects Stockdale Harrison in the first part of the 20th century. Beaumont Hall had a fine garden developed by the owner Mr Brice, a keen amateur gardener who had formed the water garden, sunken garden, Japanese, sand and the limestone gardens. It is a beautiful extensive garden, including National Plant collections; involved in research, educational visits and in recent years 'Sculpture in the Garden' during the summer.

Mile Straight; the result of canalising the river in 1889-90

In Evington there is a thirteenth century church of St. Denys with a spire that forms a focal point to the village.

An interesting solution to a large open space in the centre of Knighton Conservation area is the developing arboretum of the University of Leicester. Adjacent is the old Hall of the Knighton Estate which is now the Vice-Chancellor's residence, with 17th century origins but extensive enlargements made in the Victorian period. The façade of Knighton Hall, attributed to the architect John Johnson, looks towards the new Attenborough arboretum.

Knighton Hall, façade by John Johnson, now the official residence of the Vice Chancellor of the University of Leicester, seen from the new Attenborough arboretum

The partially sighted have responded positively to the Leicester & Wycliffe Society's Resources Centre for the Blind on Gedding Road, Evington, designed by Douglas Smith Stimson Partnership Ltd in 1988. It avoided corridors and the spaces were articulated by careful selection of floor textures, bold mouldings to identify openings, soft edges to projecting counters, together with sensitive use of tone contrasts for the colour scheme. Louis Hellman wrote in the Architects' Journal complimenting the design and concluded: 'The architects great gift is or should be imagination - not in terms of conjuring up ever novel forms but in making the leap to put ourselves in others' shoes (or wheelchairs)'.

To the north of the city centre is Abbey Park and Belgrave. St. Peter's Belgrave has an interesting Norman southern doorway. The church is set in a quiet area, an oasis away from the busy A6 Loughborough Road. It makes an interesting visual group with Belgrave Hall; a Queen Anne House built in 1713 by Edward Cradock and a little later the public park of the former gardens of Belgrave House. The Hall is now part of the Leicester Museum and has a fine collection of the furniture of Ernest Gimson, Leicester's leading Arts and Craft architect and furniture designer. These two Georgian

Belgrave Hall, and a fine example of a formal garden,
1713, now part of Leicester Museums

Belgrave House is of 1776

St Barnabus Library 1937 by Maurice Pike

Interior of the Resources Centre for the Leicester & Wycliffe Society for the Blind 1988. Architects Douglas Smith Stimson Partnership Ltd

buildings of local red brick enclose the space behind. The Hall has a significant eighteenth century garden comprising consecutive walled gardens and formal flowerbeds. Abbey Park is a large area of public open space close to the city centre and contains what little remains of the ruins of the Augustinian Abbey. To the north west of the Abbey are the windowed walls of Cavendish House built in the 1600s. From the park, we can see the new National Space Centre, adjacent to the Museum of Technology. Originally the Abbey Pumping Station of 1891, it still displays the large beam engines in an elaborate interior. It is true that we no longer build like the Victorians, but it is a reminder of the Industrial Heritage of the city and its modern manufacturing base.

The National Space Centre is a modern landmark and has become a major tourist attraction in this new millennium. The competition-winning scheme by Nicholas Grimshaw and Partners is a landmark Millennium project for the East Midlands. The rocket tower cladding inflated triple-layered panels of ethylene tetrafluoroethylene (ETFE) is 42 metres high with a mast climbing lift to give good views of the rockets. It was built on a brownfield site on the banks of the River Soar and has made use of the redundant vast drainage tanks. The building has a planetarium and a Challenger Learning Centre, primarily but not exclusively for children. It was the first outside North America where the idea of people experiencing space travel started. The same architects are also responsible for the design of the Eden Project in Cornwall.

National Space Centre 2001 by
Nicholas Grimshaw & Partners for the
University of Leicester and Leicester
City Council

An impression of the new theatre complex
Rafael Vinoly architects for Leicester City Council

The City
in the future

When I arrived in the city in the middle of the last century, it would have been reasonable to say Leicester was as its motto implied. This is what Kenneth Browne, features editor of 'The Architectural Review' said about Leicester in the 1960s.

Semper Eadem: always the same. Leicester's motto sums up the city to an outsider; the first view inevitably feels flat. There are no high spots, no dramatic sites and gestures and no obviously endearing local traits. Only later does he realise the deep and lasting virtues that are the other side of 'semper eadem'; an unhysterical balance, a willingness to accept new ideas, and a fair hearing for all points of view. These qualities have produced remarkable things – the first modern public library, a first-rate museum, first-rate schools, a city almost without slums and with perhaps the highest average standard of living in the country'

Leicester at the start of the new millennium is not the same. It is a lively multi-cultural city with a changing built environment and driven by a proactive Leicester Regeneration Company.

Mandy Stewart, Chief Executive, Leicester Haymarket Theatre describes the design of the new 'Performing Arts Centre'. 'There was an enthusiastic response to the brief by architects Rafael Vinoly and his team. It will be a unique building with the stage at street level and two performing spaces operating side by side; visually exciting by day and night and fully engaging with the community.'

I have attempted to illustrate the position as it appears to me. However, major institutions and groups will shape our city of the future. There are two significant Universities with major expansion plans. The community is requiring extensive leisure facilities. Industry, commerce and retail will change the scene. Religious communities, too, will share a burden of responsibility to enhance and build upon the rich heritage of the city at the beginning of the new millennium.

Belvoir Castle, ancestral home of the
Duke and Duchess of Rutland

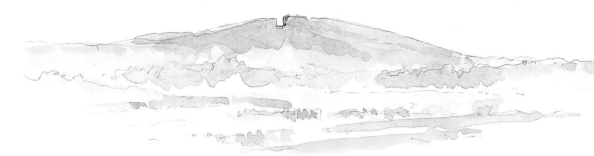

Leicestershire Rutland

'"Britain is a world by itself"; its mountains are not high, nor its rivers long, but within a few hundred miles of travel from east to west an Englishman may see more variety of scenery than are found in many bigger countries.'

A.E.Trueman

This is a quotation from his book, Geology and Scenery in England and Wales; however on a small scale this applies to Leicestershire and Rutland. Hence many travellers on the main line trains and the motorway are not aware of the rich diversity of scenery and architecture that can be found in this small and unique part of the country, by travelling east to west.

The scenery divides into three parts with the central low lying relatively flat land of the Soar Valley, flanked to the east by the 'Stone Belt' and to the west by the Charnwood Forest, the old coalfields that are now being transformed as part of the 'National Forest'.

The earliest small dwellings and barns were timber framed with wattle and daub panels frequently painted to give the 'black and white' houses. The 'A' frame was simple and stable but restricted the interior and the larger buildings adopted a frame with vertical members; diagonal bracing was incorporated to give stability and adds to the visual interest. Later brick became the infill panel. Examples of these buildings are found throughout the two counties.

Quenby Hall fine 17th Century house

The Soar Valley

In this valley to the north and south of Leicester, are the industrial towns and villages associated with the 'industrial revolution' and the communication network.

There are two castles, one in Leicester and the other in Kirby Muxloe. The latter started by Lord Hastings was never finished. Work stopped when he was executed in 1483 leaving the keep and the one tower.

An extensive number of village churches are to be found; St. Lukes Gaddesby is perhaps the most beautiful one together with St. Peter at Claybrook with the impressive Decorated Chancel dating from 1340. A superb slender, elegant needle spire, surmounting the pink granite tower of St. Mary's, Queniborough, can be seen from the surrounding countryside. There are good examples from the eighteenth century at St John the Baptist, Kings Norton and St. Peter, Gaulby.

Pevsner describes Quenby Hall as 'the most important early 17th century house in the County....built for George Ashby....dated 1620 on the clock'. It is an impressive red brick structure with stone dressings, diaper pattern of dark blue bricks. The house is built on a conventional 'H' plan.

Scraptoft Hall, with imposing iron screen and gates built in the 1700s was until recently part of De Montfort University. The Queen Anne mansion stands in its own grounds next to All Saints Church, where the 19th century architect William Pearson's tomb is situated. He was one of the best known Leicester Victorian architects who was responsible for Leicester Gaol, St. George's Church, The Theatre Royal and the County Lunatic Asylum, which is now part of the University of Leicester.

In a beautiful small parkland setting is the Georgian Baggrave Hall that was rebuilt in the 1750s.

The Pilkington Library 1977-80 designed by
Faulkner-Brown, Hendry, Watkinson, Stonor

The Carillon Tower 1922-3, Loughborough
designed by Sir Walter Tapper

Near to Lutterworth is Stanford Hall, also in a beautiful park, built 1697-1700 with the Stables of 1737 making an imposing complex seen over the lake.

There are some remarkable modest domestic buildings throughout the area. Two attracted my attention: one is the beautifully maintained house built in 1678 at Kibworth Harcourt; the other one is in Willoughby Waterleys.

The University of Loughborough was founded in 1909 as a University of Technology, having strong connections with industry and latterly expanding into many fields, including sport both for research and training. The new National Cricket Academy is a fine building by David Morley architects built in 2003. The Pilkington Library 1977-80 attracted my attention, designed by Faulkner-Brown, Hendy, Watkinson, Stonor.

In the town of Loughborough is the Carillon Tower 1922-3 in Queens Park and designed by Sir Walter Tapper. It was the first Carillon to be built in Britain and said to be modelled on the belfry at Moulins France. The forty seven bells were cast in the local 'Bell Foundry'.

Queen Anne Scraptoft Hall & Gates 1700's

All Saints Church, Scraptoft

House 1693, Willoughby Waterleys

Stanford Hall 1697-1700 and Stables 1737 near Lutterworth

St Peter Gaulby rebuilt in 1741
by John Wing for Squire William Fortrey

Georgian Baggrave Hall rebuilt in the 1750's

St. Lukes, Gaddesby

House 1678, Kibworth Harcourt

West Leicestershire

The old Charnwood Forest combined with the new National Forest dominates the scene. The oldest house in the county is Bradgate House in the hunting park. Only the remains can be seen of the house the Greys built but there is sufficient to demonstrate the size and grandeur of this building constructed with diapered pattern brickwork. One can admire the impressive west wing, originally with a Great Hall and two imposing gables. It is one of the first country houses built in the country and was never landscaped. Lady Jane Grey was the young nine day Queen of England and when she was beheaded at the Tower of London in 1554 the oaks in the park had their tops removed. They are still a feature and reminder of the past. In 1748 the Greys built 'Old John' as a memorial to an old retainer of the family; it is a prominent land mark that can be seen from the city of Leicester.

Ashby Castle was started as a Norman manor house and is an example of medieval architecture. Following the Wars of the Roses, Lord Hastings, a powerful and wealthy man, received in 1474 the royal licence to fortify Ashby and Kirby because he had powerful enemies. The first use of brick after the Roman Period was found here and is beautifully maintained by English Heritage.

The Shirleys of Staunton Harold rebuilt the church in 1653 during the Cromwell period, an almost unique feat, which recorded on the plaque over the door '…..Sir Robert Shirley, Bart,…… to have done the best things in the worst time' The south elevation of the house seen from across the lake is c1770. Some claim it was originally designed by Inigo Jones.

A well maintained Gatehouse and moat was part of the 15th century Manor House but is now demolished. A fine timber framed house of the 16th century is attached to the Gatehouse at Appleby Magna.

The oaks and deer Bradgate Park

Remains of Bradgate House

Old John built by the Greys in 1748

Ashby Castle 1474.
Lord Hastings converted it from a
Norman Manor House

Church of St Mary and St Hardulph
above the lime-stone quarry, Breedon-on-the-Hill

Stoneywell Cottage, Ulverscroft 1899
designed by Ernest Gimson

Staunton Harold Church1653, south elevation of house c1770

In the next village of Appleby Parva is one of the finest early schools. The Sir John Moore school was built 1693-7. It is said to have had preliminary designs by Sir Christopher Wren, but the architect attributed to the work was Sir William Wilson. It was Sir John Moore, the benefactor, who was Lord Mayor of London and made his fortune in the East India trade.

The Church of St. Mary and St. Hardulph at Breedon-on-the-Hill has survived the quarrying adjacent; it is like a beacon on the dramatic face of the lime-stone quarry. It was originally a monastic church of between 675 and 691, but the present building dates back to the 12th century.

A house that fascinates me is Stoneywell in the Charnwood Forest, designed by Ernest Gimson in 1899 and a perfect example of nature and manmade uniting as it appears to grow out of the rocky outcrop in a timeless manner.

Sir John Moore School Appleby Parva 1693-7
designed by Sir William Wilson

Gatehouse and moat, Appleby Magna,
part of the 15th-century Manor House but now demolished

Belvoir Castle, ancestral home of
the Duke and Duchess of Rutland

Rutland and
East Leicestershire

Church of St Giles and medieval footbridge at Medbourne

This relatively small area is packed with fine buildings in beautiful countryside taking full advantage of the good soil that made clearance in the 'middle ages' easy to expose land for good productive pasture. Prosperous farms, scattered villages and small market towns sprang up. The underlying limestone and ironstone were quarried and used extensively; usually dressed and built to courses. A great variety of colour of the stones gives a rich quality to the buildings. Colly Weston slate, not a true slate but a stone that splits for roofing, gives an homogeneous effect of completeness, ensuring buildings are in harmony with the landscape in colour and tone. W.G Hoskins talks of 'delightful roofs of Colly Weston slate, their sepia warmness heightened by mosses and lichen that grows so freely in their crevices'. It is not surprising that this stone was in demand for the colleges of Cambridge.

The original Belvoir Castle was built in the thirteenth century. A formidable structure in the elevated position, it must have been awesome to the enemy and men on the flat landscape of the Vale of Belvoir. The present building was rebuilt in the nineteenth century to the plans of James Wyatt. It has been the ancestral home of the Duke and Duchess of Rutland for over one thousand years.

The Church of St. Mary's Melton Mowbray stands out to me as the finest landmark of this area and is also one of the best churches in Leicestershire and Rutland. Its size and quality reflects the prosperity here as part of the golden age of medieval England. Close by is Anne of Cleve's House, an important building in the fifteenth century; there are likely associations with Henry VIII, and it may have been the priest's house. Unfortunately it has seen many alterations and only a few original parts remain. Maison Dieu is opposite the church, founded in 1640 as an almshouse by Robert Hudson.

Foxton Locks, Victorian masterpiece of engineering of a flight of ten locks

Hallaton village green with butter cross and St Michael's Church

Anne of Cleves's House

Maison Dieu 1640 as an Almshouse by Robert Hudson

St Peter & St Paul, Great Bowden

Market Place, Market Harborough with
Church of St Dionysius & Grammar School 1614

Market Harborough has the Church of St. Dionysius with a fine spire as the focal point of the market town and the adjacent beautiful little grammar school of 1614 making an impressive Market Place. The church was originally dependent on Great Bowden, where the only burials can still take place at St. Peter and St. Paul Church. However, little remains of an earlier building.

Rutland's county town, Oakham, has a butter cross in the central square that has been on the site for more than 700 years. Its name is said to derive from the dairy products sold there. Adjacent is the fourteenth and fifteenth century Church of All Saints and the original public school building of 1584, founded by Archdeacon Johnson. Close by is the Great Hall of the remaining part of Oakham Castle or perhaps correctly named a 'fortified house'. This beautiful town lies in the fertile Vale of Catmose and near to Rutland Water.

Normanton Church at Rutland Water was saved when the area was flooded to form a massive reservoir of 3500 acres, which is also now an important bird sanctuary and water sports centre. The shores were landscaped by Dame Sylvia Crowe.

Market Square, Uppingham with Church of St Peter & St Paul

St Peter & St Paul Church at Tickencote

Yew tree avenue at Clipsham

Uppingham has a fine Market Square where the Church of St. Peter and St. Paul is situated. The famous School, like Oakham, was also founded in 1584 by Archdeacon Johnson. Pevsner says 'The buildings themselves remind us of a college more than a school - and, more specifically, a Cambridge or Oxford college.'

The churches that attracted my attention are St. Peter and St. Paul at Tickencote, with superb Norman work, the village church at Gaddesby, and the imposing Neville Holt complex where Opera is performed in the grounds during the summer. In the village of Queniborough there are some fine old buildings and the Church of St. Mary's with a pink granite low tower surmounted by the fine tall needle like spire that can be seen from afar. Hallaton is a peaceful village with a large green, butter cross and St. Michael's Church. In contrast there are two beautiful eighteenth century churches at Gaulby and Kings Norton.

We find at Foxton Locks on the Grand Union Canal fascinating Victorian engineering with 'incline planes' and 10 locks to negotiate. The Museum tells the story of the canals in Britain, including working models.

There are many fine houses in Rutland and East Leicestershire arising from a long tradition of successful productive farming, strategic location, good communications to near-by cities and London, with an abundance of stunning countryside to choose from.

Burley-on-the-Hill was built in a superb location on the site of an older establishment between 1694 and 1708. Daniel Finch, second Earl of Nottingham may have been his own architect. John Lumley from Northhampton supervised the work. An impressive structure over-looking Rutland Water, the house has an imposing main entrance façade to the north with a curved Doric colonnade.

Neville Holt

Oakham central square with All Saints Church, buttercross and Public School 1584

Burley-on-the-Hill, 1694-1708 by Daniel Finch second Earl of Nottingham

Bede House, Liddington, one wing of the original
medieval rural palace of the Bishop of Lincoln

Bede House, Liddington, is the one wing of the original medieval rural palace of the Bishop of Lincoln that has been beautifully restored by English Heritage. There is a fine Church adjacent which is also a focus for musical concerts.

Dingley Hall started as a manor house for an unknown Knight of the Order of St. John of Jerusalem in 1135. However it has been enlarged and changed many times. The beautiful south front was built in 1684. The Porch is the only surviving part of the Edward Griffin House dated 1558 which was later repositioned and forms the entrance to The Porch House home of 'Music at Dingley'.

It is interesting to find that 'The Pastures', now Pastures House by C.F.A.Voysey, was built in 1902 for the present owner's great aunt. The house has many of the characteristics both inside and out that made the work of this architect influential at the turn of the last century. Hence many of the features of the designs by Voysey have continued to inspire domestic architecture around the country.

A remarkable engineering structure is to be found between Harringworth and Seaton: Welland Viaduct was constructed between 1876 and 1878 to carry the LMS Kettering to Manton branch line. At the time it was perhaps difficult to accept the 'shock of the new', but it has since become a beloved element in the landscape and now stands as a monument to railway architecture.

Rutland Water is a great lake that in addition to its many sporting facilities is a rich wildlife habitat. The bird sanctuary is vital to all fauna, but is critical to birds on their migration flights across continents. They are global indicators of national and international policies of nature conservation. Rutland Water and the new National Forest are two good examples of positive action locally to protect and enhance wildlife habitats and nature conservation for future generations.

Having explored Rutland and East Leicestershire travelling along twisting roads in beautiful countryside and recording in paintings and sketches many fine buildings, discovering exquisite villages and towns, I have concluded that much is little; the motto of Rutland 'Multum In Parvo'.

The Porch 1558 repositioned from original location of the earlier
house of Dingley Hall and it is now part of the Porch House

South front of Dingley Hall 1684

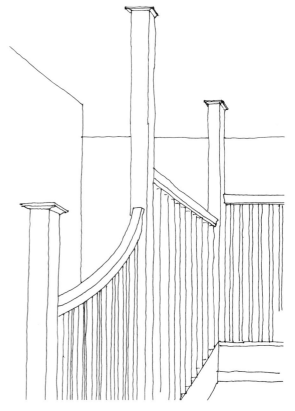

Small clock tower in the stable yard and the internal
staircase are characteristic designs of C F A Voysey

'The Pastures' now Pastures House,
by C F A Voysey, 1902 in North Luffenham.

Welland Viaduct, between Harringworth & Seaton 1876 -1878

Return of the Osprey, Rutland Water

Normanton Church at Rutland Water

Conclusion

I have made a search for old buildings that have attracted my attention and chosen from the new what I consider good and will stand the test of time. The 'shock of the new' will not deter them from becoming part of our heritage and they will possibly join favourites from the past.

We must protect the good without prejudice, remembering that not all old buildings must be preserved. Conservation is not the same as preservation. It is important for designers of the future to encourage good new buildings, gardens and landscapes.

I am certain the City and the two Counties can look forward with the enthusiastic knowledge that there will be many exciting new buildings and gardens in the future; there is already the new National Forest and the new theatre in the City to give optimism for the future.

I am content if the book conveys in paintings and sketches a record to match the words of Lord Attenborough – 'reflects its historic past, rejoices in the diversity of its present and heralds its optimism for the future'. Originally these words were applied to Leicester but can equally apply to Leicestershire and Rutland.

The delicate wild rose

We live in a fragile world, our aim must be to move towards a zero-waste society. Locally there are research programmes at the universities on Energy and Sustainable Development. The local authorities are increasing the awareness and implementing policies on environmental issues. Leicester was Britain's first Environment City.

The vision of Environ, Leicester, 'A society where every individual and organisation is contributing to an increasingly sustainable environment. Think global, act local.'

Index and Glossary

Buildings, places, architects, artists & designers
Page numbers in Italics indicate illustrations